STEPPARENTING

50 One-Minute DOs and DON'Ts for Stepdads and Stepmoms

By

Randall Hicks

WORDSLINGER PRESS
San Diego, California

Printed in the United States of America

ISBN: 978-0-9794430-3-9 (trade paperback)
ISBN: 978-0-9794430-4-6 (ebook format)

Wordslinger Press
9921 Carmel Mountain Road, Suite 335
San Diego, CA 92129

PUBLISHER'S NOTE: This publication is designed to provide helpful information in regard to the subject matter covered. It is sold with the understanding that the author and publisher are not engaged in rendering legal or counseling services. Legal and parenting issues discussed herein can be advised about differently, and what is helpful advice for one person may not be helpful for another. If you require legal or family counseling advice, you should seek the services of a licensed professional to serve your personal and unique needs.

Library of Congress Cataloging-in-Publication Data

Names: Hicks, Randall, 1956- author.
Title: Stepparenting : 50 one-minute dos and don'ts for stepdads and stepmoms
/ by Randall Hicks.
Description: San Diego : WordSlinger Press, 2016.
Identifiers: LCCN 2016036067| ISBN 9780979443039 (trade pbk.) | ISBN 9780979443046 (ebook)
Subjects: LCSH: Stepfamilies. | Stepparents--Psychology. | Stress (Psychology) | Parenting.
Classification: LCC HQ759.92 .H53 2016 | DDC 306.874/7--dc23
LC record available at https://lccn.loc.gov/2016036067

Table of Contents

Do show love and respect for your spouse.

Kids - even in their most self-centered moments - secretly want to see their parents be happy. If you are the new man or woman in the life of one of the child's existing parents, nothing will impress a child more than seeing you love and respect their parent.

Remember also that as the parent and stepparent, you are the two key role models in what a marriage should look like, and how spouses treat each other. The "silent lessons" you give in your daily actions will have a much larger impact on your child's life than when sitting down for important lectures.

Don't use chores as punishment.

Children will learn to hate work around the house if it's seen as punishment. Yes, the yard may need to be raked, the house vacuumed, or the after-dinner dishes washed, but don't make it punishment. When those activities are chores, fine. But as punishment? No. It may be particularly resented if the punishment is assigned by the stepparent.

A great way to build a good work ethic in a child, and additionally to create a family activity, is to start a family chore day. Maybe once or twice a month you set aside half a day on a Saturday to clean up the yard or the house, or clean out the garage. As the children work side by side with you they see you keep a happy attitude as you work, with a measurable goal to be accomplished, such as a pristine yard when you are done. And add a reward in the end, like

2

everyone going to a movie together, so the concept of "good work brings rewards" is subconsciously planted.

Don't yell.

Yes, we all lose our temper from time to time and yell, and there may even be times where it's needed. But generally it's not the route to take. Have you ever been yelled at by a parent, boss, teacher, friend or whomever? Was your reaction, "Oh, thanks for yelling. Now I *really* want to listen to you." Likely, no. It actually has the opposite effect.

Yelling usually accomplishes nothing but a release of your own anger, and as the stepparent, your words will be judged more harshly than those of the existing parent. So be the calm voice in the storm, and don't give your stepchild an excuse to find fault with you. Adopt the old "count to ten" rule before you react, and give yourself a moment to calm down and think about what you are going to say.

Also, by example you can teach a very valuable lesson in how you react in stressful or difficult situations. *It's easy to be nice when everything is going our way. But our real character shows when we are facing adversity or stress.* So it is at times like these that a parent must strive to be at their best. If your child learns this lesson as well, it will be a benefit to them their entire life in how they interact with others.

DO choose activities that bond you as a family.

Finding things you enjoy doing together is critical to family bonding. And although watching TV or going to a movie together are fine activities, the problem with them is they are not really interactive.

Strive for activities that will involve conversation and/or interaction. This might be outside activities like playing catch, hiking, ping pong, bike riding, or inside activities like board games, cooking, a small art or construction project, or creative activities like Legos or K'Nex.

Don't hide every parental disagreement.

It's often said "don't argue in front of the kids," and that's not a bad rule. However, it would be setting an unmatchable example if a child never sees a single disagreement between parenting figures. A child needs to learn disagreements are a normal part of life, whether it be with a friend or a spouse.

Seeing a disagreement can actually be instructive if the child sees you remain respectful of each other, and witnesses you work through a disagreement and resolve the issue. The message is "Yes, people disagree and don't always get their way, but they can respectfully talk about those issues and try to resolve them."

7

Don't buy love.

Buying a gift gives everyone immediate gratification. The child gets a cool gift and is happy, at least for the moment. And you are happy too, not just in seeing the happiness in the child, but likely also (if you are honest with yourself) thrilled with the gratitude that flows back to you. But it's "fast food" gratification.

Gifts are great, but if they are given at the wrong time, or for inappropriate reasons, they are transparent efforts to buy affection from the child. Eventually, both the child, and your spouse, will see it for what it is.

Do give time.

Time is usually our most precious commodity, thus the hardest to give up. The reality is, simply giving a child a present or special treat of some type is much easier than finding free time in a day already filled with a job and household chores, not to mention needing some time for yourself.

But part of parenting is sacrifice. Your stepchild may not give you any credit for it, but you taking part in the thankless tasks that go with parenting (driving the child to his or her various activities, helping with homework, coaching their sports team, attending parent-teacher conferences, sitting at the Girl Scout cookie table in front of the grocery store, or even just giving them your complete and undivided attention while at the dinner table) are the kind of actions that will be recognized and remembered as time goes on. If you honestly want to be a true parent to your stepchild, try your best to commit to these activities as much as the existing parent.

Don't point out your own attributes.

Every parent has been there - feeling like you are doing too much for others, sometimes particularly for your stepchild, and there is no reciprocity or appreciation coming your way. It is even easier to feel this resentment as a stepparent because part of you might secretly think, "I don't *have* to be here. Doesn't everyone know I voluntarily became a stepparent and took on these responsibilities?"

This is never more true than when facing the "I am the center of the universe" mentality of most children. It's so easy to want to tell your stepchild the growing list in your head of all that you do for them, usually not thanked or noticed.

But don't fall into that trap. The problem is the "small world" view of a child, and just the way their brains work at younger ages. Kids simply don't have an understanding of the big picture of life, or the world, so naturally put themselves in the center.

There are two specific things you can do to help them see beyond their little world, with them as the sun and everything circling around them. One is to broaden your child's awareness of the world, the unspoken message being that we are each a very small part of something much bigger, in both good and bad ways.

For example, when a news story comes on TV about a catastrophic event like a flood or tornado wiping out entire cities, with families left homeless, invite your child to watch with you (but without turning it into a "how lucky we are by comparison" lecture). And also share joyous and magnificent events with them, such as watching surfers on a monster wave, or watching the sunrise and talk about how it is rising all over the world at different times, waking up billions of people.

A more direct way to create more awareness in their home life is to bring up family contributions without referencing them specifically to you. Instead, ask, "What more do you think I should be doing for your mom?" Then, "And how about you? What more could you be doing for your mom to make her life easier. She works really hard for all of us."

Don't try to be the cool parent.

It's easy to want to get on a child's good side by letting them "get away" with stuff, particularly when you are the stepparent looking for a way inside your stepchild's barriers. But letting kids slide on rules and responsibilities, or identifying with their point of view even when it's inappropriate, is an easy trap to fall into.

Yes, parents and stepparents can be friends to a child, but they are parents first. So when the child's behavior is unsafe (wanting to skateboard or ride their bike in the dark), or unkind (telling a "funny" story about a child getting bullied or ridiculed at school), you need to step in and let them know what's right, even if it's not what the child wants to hear. Your child needs your guidance on what is proper behavior and what is not, and in the long term will respect you for trying to teach that.

DO be fair and consistent in discipline.

When families merge, there are often conflicting styles of discipline. It's confusing for a child to have one standard in their past, and a new one when a stepparent joins the family. And sometimes the situation for a child is quadrupled, as perhaps both existing parents find new partners, now there are two families, each with one existing parent and one stepparent.

Work with not just your spouse, but also the out-of-house parent, to find common styles of discipline and consistent consequences. Hopefully he or she will understand this will not only help the child, but all of you as well.

And what is considered permissible behavior should be the same for both boys and girls, not a different standard based upon gender. Also, the same standard should be applied whether the child is your stepchild or your existing child.

Don't spank.

If spanking is part of your discipline, the stepparent should not be the one doing the spanking. There are too many potential problems stemming from spanking to add to the burden of being a stepparent. So if spanking must be a part of your discipline, have it done only by the existing parent.

There is an interesting debate on the correctness of spanking among those seeking biblical support. Spanking supporters cite Old Testament verses like Proverbs 13:24 ("He that spares his rod hates his son: but he that loves him chastens him early.").

But non-spanking Christians point out that the Old Testament is filled with many stories of violence which are not meant to impart parenting advice. For example, Exodus 21:15 says "If anyone curses his father or mother, he must be put to death." Every child in the world at one point badmouths their parents, yet we clearly don't find biblical support to kill them. Yet many still feel "sparing the rod," is biblical support for spanking.

Non-spanking advocates also point out that the New Testament is "non-spanking." We see that Jesus sought to modify behavior with only kindness and love. He discouraged the Old Testament "eye for an eye" and taught "turn the other cheek." As said in Corinthians 4:21, "What do you prefer? Shall I come to you with a whip, or in love with a gentle spirit?" So the question to be asked is if there is really biblical support for spanking when looking at the Bible as a whole?

Also, laws and perceptions have changed drastically in the last few decades. For example, many people of parenting age can remember that when they were kids, "swats" were freely administered to students by public school officials. Yet nowadays taking a wooden paddle to a child's buttocks by a teacher in most states would likely not only cost them their job, but perhaps even result in criminal charges.

Don't wait until marriage to start taking on a role.

The transition of you as a "mom's boyfriend" or "dad's girlfriend" into a stepparent will be smoother if you've assumed some parenting-style roles prior to "the job" officially beginning with marriage or cohabitation. These can be small actions, like bringing the child to or from school or sport practices, helping with homework, cooking for the family, et cetera.

Even better, let the child see you taking an active role to help their existing parent with their personal tasks. So if you are a future stepdad and your wife-to-be struggles to find time in the day to work at her job, transport her child, do the housework and tend to the garden, pitch in around the house or yard on a weekend, rather than just coming over for a date.

Do go slow.

Let's face it. Your spouse chose you - the child did not. So although you have won the heart of your new spouse, you are starting from step one with their child. So go slow and don't rush the relationship.

Let the child take the lead on when to expand into new activities, such as those with just the child and stepparent, whether it's going to the movies, or doing a sports activity. Don't hesitate to gently express your interest in such outings, but don't get defensive if the initial answer is no.

Do let your spouse and his or her child have their own private time.

In a desire to create a new family, sometimes it's easy to go overboard and want to do every activity together. There is nothing wrong, however, with the child wanting - and needing - some private time and activities with just their existing parent. As the stepparent, show your support for your spouse and the child to have some private time.

Do create new family activities and traditions.

Talk to your spouse about selecting some new activities that will be unique to your newly formed family. Not only are original activities fun for a child, but it will help keep him or her from comparing the same activity done previously with the out-of-house parent.

These activities need not necessarily be "big" ones, such as going to an expensive amusement park or weekend getaways. It might simply be Friday night pizza, Sunday breakfasts at a favorite restaurant, or taking up soccer or frisbee-tossing. These "small" activities have the extra benefit of not having any of the pressure and stress that accompanies big events like vacations.

Do get ready for "You are not my dad/mom."

These words can be hurtful, and it's okay if your stepchild sees a moment of pain on your face that you can't quite hide when you hear them. You have feelings too. But you have to avoid getting defensive. Your reaction should be to agree, "You're right. I'm not your biological mom. But we live in the same house, we both love your dad, and I care about you too. I guess I just can't help but act like your mom sometimes."

What is often really happening, particularly if the parent you have replaced is still active in the child's life, is the child may feel it would be disrespectful to their out-of-house parent to show you too much love. You can help resolve this by never making it appear you are in competition with the out-of-house parent. Speak positively of that parent and show your support for their relationship.

Don't expect an immediate blended family.

Popular TV shows of the past like *The Brady Bunch* and *Step By Step* present a fictional stepfamily bliss that is unmatchable in real life. If your stepchild was very young when your stepparenting began, then the child may see you on a par with the existing parent. However, if your relationship starts when the child is older, you may start off being seen as "the guest who never leaves."

This can be quite unnerving for you, but from the perspective of your stepchild, that may honestly be how he or she initially views you. Think about how you would feel if your spouse were to announce to you that his or her brother was going to move in with you, have the right to tell you what to do, and stay for the next ten or fifteen years. You had no real voice in the decision, yet it affects your life every moment you live in your home. It's easy to see how your arrival could be viewed in the same way in the eyes of a child.

So don't get frustrated. Avoid the expectation of an "instant family," and recognize that just like it took time to win the affection of your new spouse, similar efforts will be needed to "win over" the child. In time, your sincere heart will be recognized.

Don't be jealous when the child talks about the out-of-house parent.

Be supportive when the child wants to talk about past times with the out-of-house parent. When you overhear, "Mom, remember that fun weekend with dad when we all went to visit grandma and grandpa at the cabin," show your interest in their past experiences, rather than expect everyone to pretend there were never any happy moments before the child's parents' relationship ended.

And if the parent you replaced is deceased, understand the desire of the family to keep up prior family photos in

27

places of honor, like the family room wall, side by side with photos of you with the newly created family. Having reminders, and openly talking about the deceased parent, shows the child that you as a stepparent understand the important role the parent played and that you want to keep their memory alive in the household.

Don't let your stepchild's rudeness go unnoticed.

Although it's wise to not react to every potentially offensive comment, and letting a few comments roll off your back is necessary in family life, that does not mean that every act of rudeness should be ignored in a quest for household harmony.

Sometimes a consequence or discipline for a child's conduct or attitude is needed. However, when the issue is solely "attitude," often a comment or question is enough. Ideally this should be something that puts the ball back in the court of your stepchild, such as, "I'm not yelling or getting angry at you, so why are you yelling at me? Come back when you can talk as politely to me as I am talking to you."

The example you show will teach your stepchild how to handle stress and conflict by the fact you don't react with apathy, anger or cruelty, rather show caring, calmness and fairness.

Do find time to focus on your spouse.

It's easy for all parents to get too focused on the child and let the marriage slowly crumble with neglect. This can be a trap even easier to fall into for second families, as a parent may feel bad about the first relationship failing and wanting to "make it up" to the child, thus focusing more on the child than the marriage.

But the new relationship will also crumble if it is not nourished. Also, you are also setting an example for your child they will carry into their own marriage one day, so openly loving and nurturing your spouse will help both your marriage and your child.

So whether it's an official date night or just taking a walk together after dinner, find some consistent one-on-one time with your spouse. And make sure the "time together" includes a little romance. Little signs of affection at random, perhaps even unexpected moments, go a long way to keep romance alive - a lingering kiss on the back of your spouse's neck while he or she is cooking, a back rub while reading or watching TV.

And speaking of kissing, when was the last time you had a prolonged passionate kiss (more than five seconds, the kind that would embarrass your kids if they saw it) with your spouse that wasn't during sex? Such kisses are not just for the bedroom.

Do accept your stepchild for who they are.

You as a stepparent may have genetic gifts or interests that are completely different from your stepchild's. You may like sports, yet your stepchild prefers to read. Or you are an academic but your stepchild has little interest in anything not involving a ball to throw, kick or hit. Maybe you are confident and outgoing and your stepchild is quiet and shy.

Share your interests and maybe the child will embrace them, but if not, accept it in good cheer and sincerely support the unique interests of your stepchild. Let your stepchild overhear you bragging to others about their special skills and accomplishments, whatever they might be.

Do take care of yourself.

The very fact you are reading this book shows you are committed toward your stepchild. That may also mean you are like many parents who spend so much time and energy taking care of their spouse and stepchild, that you forget about yourself. Doing this too often, for too long, can actually set a bad example in your family that a parent has no life outside the house and work, and it can also lead to some resentment on your part as the years go on.

So remember that it's okay to take an afternoon off now and then to do what gives you peace of mind and pleasure, whether it's just some alone time, or a day out with friends for lunch or some tennis or yoga. Just as you support your new family, they should support you.

Do find "little" activities to do together.

When you think back on some of your most memorable moments with family members, it is likely not a big vacation or huge event. It was more likely little moments, like making homemade cookies with your mom, or playing catch in the backyard with your dad. So fill your life with many such "little" events and activities, most of them costing you nothing and requiring no advance planning. Toss a frisbee, teach the dog some tricks, decorate cupcakes, build a birdhouse...

DO build a family website or Facebook page.

It's the rare child who does not like being on a computer, regardless of their age. Propose starting a family Facebook page or website to post photos and thoughts to share with friends and relatives. Just type "free websites" in a search engine line Google to find the countless free website options available, or consider a social media like Facebook. Neither option requires much in the way of computer skills, but does allow a lot of creativity on the part of you and your stepchild. Taking pictures, selecting which ones to use and what stories and adventures to share can be fun.

Don't get sucked into choosing sides between stepchildren.

It's common for both husband and wife to each bring one or more children into the new blended family. And it's guaranteed that like in any sibling relationship, there will be some arguments and friction between the kids. This usually results in the child seeking the support of their existing parent.

Try to avoid feeling you always need to be the problem solver. Instead, avoid taking sides and frame their argument for them as you see it, and give them a framework in which to resolve the issue themselves. "So Jessica, you're mad because Suzie gets in the bathroom first in the morning and you think she takes too long. And

Suzie, you are mad because Jessica is banging on the door and bothering you when you feel it's your time in the bathroom. How about you two talk it out and give me a solution during dinner."

Many times there is no significant dispute to resolve, just typical childhood emotions and tension that is natural when sharing space. Also, simply letting the moment of tension pass is often enough to diffuse the dispute. With time, and the realization that neither the existing parent nor stepparent is going to crumble, kids get the idea they are expected to solve their own disputes. The arguments won't completely disappear, but gradually the parent and stepparent get dragged into fewer of them.

DO consider stepparent adoption.

Many stepfamilies involve both committed moms and dads, and even though the relationship between them failed, both parents share a deep love and involvement with the child. In such cases, stepparent adoption would not be appropriate. But sometimes one parent was never involved, can't be found or has abandoned their parenting role. (Statistically this is more often the birth father.) When this is the case, and as the stepparent you are the only mom or dad figure in the child's life, you may wish to consider stepparent adoption.

This means you will no longer legally be "step" mom or "step" dad, and instead officially become just "mom" or "dad," which is likely what the child is already calling you anyway. From a legal point of view, it typically means the adopting stepparent is fully assuming all parental responsibility, as if the child was born to him or her, and relieving the absent parent of future responsibility and child support. If the adopting stepparent is the father, the child often legally assumes his last name as part of the adoption.

The child sees that your commitment to him or her is now for life, taking on the legal obligation of them as your child, as if he or she were born to you. Many children see this as truly becoming a family, as acts speak louder than words.

So if the out-of-house parent is a fully absent one and your relationship with both spouse and child is a strong one, consider making your stepchild your legal child. So rather than saying "I think of you as my son/daughter," you can truly say "You are my son/daughter." It is the same difference as marrying your spouse, as opposed to forever just cohabiting and saying "You are like a wife to me."

Do give easy opportunities to talk.

Some children enjoy an official "family talk time," such as "pass the spoon" where the spoon holder gets to give their thoughts without fear of consequences in a family roundtable.

But other kids may feel it is too forced to share their feelings in such a formal "talk" session, and find it much easier when doing everyday activities (while working together to prepare dinner, setting the table, washing the dishes afterwards, driving to school, et cetera). Mealtimes are also an excellent time to share, so it's a great policy to keep the TV and cellphones off while you eat. Lives can be hectic and busy, but try to select at least one meal a day that is shared as a family and isn't rushed.

DO be flexible in what your stepchild calls you.

You might be hoping for "Mom" or "Dad," but that might be unrealistic if the child has a continuing role with his or her out-of-house mom or dad. And that's okay. Using your first name, which is what they hear their existing parent and all your friends call you, is fine and should not be seen as rude. This is because you are family. If you were an uncle or aunt, for example, you'd be "Uncle Bob" or "Aunt Carolyn," not "sir" or "ma'am." And sometimes, even if it takes years to accomplish, the use of a first name can slowly evolve into "Mom" or "Dad" in their vocabulary.

A child may even come up with his or her own affectionate nickname for you, like "D-2" for Dad Number Two, but want to reserve "Mom" and "Dad" for their existing parents.

Some kids call both the out-of-house parent and stepparent "mom" or "dad" and give the name double duty, which is a big compliment to the stepparent if the child elects to do so.

The key is not the label you are given, it's the role you fill. What is a mom or a dad after all anyway? A mentor. A guide through life. A safety net. A friend. You can be all those things even if you never get the "Mom" or "Dad" label.

Do recognize adult stepchildren have emotions too.

Just because stepchildren are adults and out of the house when you marry their existing parent doesn't mean you won't have a huge impact upon the family's happiness and success. They are the children of your new spouse, and likely the center of your spouse's universe.

So consider their feelings, and understand that you entering their family is as big an event for them as it is for you. It might take them time to fully trust and accept you, but seeing you make their existing parent happy will go a long way to accomplishing this.

They may also fear that the marriage will lose them an anticipated inheritance, with a parent's estate going to the new spouse rather than to the children. It is best to directly address these issues so the adult children know where they stand.

Do consider attending worship together.

Whether you are Presbyterian, Catholic, Mormon, Jewish, Buddhist, Muslim or ?, worshiping as a family can be beneficial. And if you are a family without a faith, remember that virtually every mainstream religion has the basic tenets of honesty and kindness toward others as principal values, certainly part of something you'd like your child to be exposed to.

If family worship wasn't something the family did previously, this could have the added benefit of being one of those new activities you are doing which is unique to your newly formed family. And your day of worship can include small traditions that are fun, such as a big Sunday breakfast at a restaurant, or just stopping for donuts on the way home.

Don't get upset on Mother's/Father's Day.

Mother's Day and Father's Day can be awkward occasions for a stepparent. The child may look only to their existing mom or dad as the one deserving special acknowledgment, which can be hurtful if it is you doing the thankless tasks day in and day out that warrant the special considerations of the day. And even for existing parents, most kids don't understand the specialness of the day for parents. To them, it's just another holiday that has little meaning.

It's up to your spouse to talk to the child about acknowledging your role. There is nothing wrong with two moms or two dads getting separate special acknowledgments. And don't feel bad if you need to tell your spouse about your feelings because he or she doesn't notice it on their own. They may not realize how left out you feel.

Don't push gender-specific roles on your spouse.

A wife might think discipline is the man's job, while a man may feel discussing emotional issues with a child is a woman's job. Not only are such generalizations wrong simply based upon gender, they can also be counterproductive, particularly in a stepfamily. One reality to be aware of, however, is that initially a child will best accept discipline and nurturing from the existing parent. With time, as a stepfamily gels, all parental roles can hopefully be shared.

Gender equity not only helps your child within your family, but with life in general. Children will see first-hand that they are not limited to stereotypical roles: that dads can cook and clean and nurture, and that moms can pay the bills, be the primary wage-earner and be great at sports.

DO be prepared to pay for the failures of the out-of-house parent.

When a parent fails to show for visitation, or otherwise disappoints the child, don't be surprised if your stepchild finds you to blame. You have to understand the child needs a reason other than "Dad's a flake," or "Mom must not want to see me anymore." The disappointment they feel often needs to be directed at someone and in a way it's a compliment they trust you to be recipient and "safe harbor" for their anger.

It's tempting to want to want to vocalize your criticisms of the absent parent to the child at these moments, but it's often best left unsaid. Even if the child secretly agrees with any criticism you might make, he or she will likely not want to hear it from you. It's like your spouse insulting your parents. You might agree, but you don't want to hear it from anyone's lips but your own. Also, some kids will see your disrespect for the out-of-house parent as disrespect for the child himself or herself, as the child of a "bad" parent.

So within limits, just take your lumps and hang in there. In time, the child will see the out-of-house parent's behavior for what it is, and recognize they must lower their expectations. By comparison, however, over time a child will usually recognize your presence and support the entire time.

And try not to secretly root for the out-of-house parent's failure, thinking it will just make your life easier if he or she were out of the picture. To the contrary, do all you can to keep the out-of-house parent's role with the child a viable and positive one, as it is the child who will gain the benefits or suffer the loss.

Do help your stepchild feel good about himself/herself.

Why do we choose certain people as our friends? Why do we want to spend time with some people more than others? The answer is usually quite simple. *We like to be around people who make us feel good about ourselves.* People we can trust. People who are reliable, honest and kind.

That small piece of wisdom is priceless in making friends with anyone, particularly your stepchild. Be positive. Be real. Be sincere. Be consistent. Be available.

Don't feel you need to solve every problem.

Whether you hear it from your spouse, or directly from your stepchild, you will be told of problems that the child is going through in that long and difficult voyage through childhood. It's a sad fact that kids can be particularly cruel toward each other, especially "girl on girl." The natural reaction for well-meaning parents is to provide a solution to the problem. And if it is the kind of a problem a parent can solve, great.

But usually it's the kind of upsetting situation that sometimes occurs in a child's world, such as another child's hurtful comments, or being left out of some activities or friendships. This makes your heart ache for your child, but you know to insert yourself in every such situation will likely only be detrimental to your child down the road, particularly in their relationships with those other children they will have to interact with at school or in the neighborhood.

Kids intuitively know this, and don't necessarily want you to try to make every problem go away. But you can absolutely help in several ways: 1) You can be the sympathetic listener; 2) You can teach empowerment; and 3) You can teach a philosophy of life. These can all help not just now, but in the years ahead. Let's look at these three specific options:

A sympathetic and patient ear, listening without interruption, or a caring hug, is sometimes all a child really needs and wants. And you can show empathy by sharing a story about yourself at their age, when you went through the same thing. The unspoken words being "I'm here and happy, so I survived it. So will you."

You also want to empower your child. A helpful lifelong philosophy to teach is "Don't let other people take your happiness away." The reality is that most "mean" people are secretly unhappy themselves, and this seems to motivate them to take it away from others. A child's understanding of this can help.

Also, share the importance of your child's own inner strength and personal choices in how to react when things don't go as we want. Everyone in the world has asked "Why do bad things happen to good people?" Your child needs to know that he or she is not exempt from the "sometimes bad things happen in life" reality.

Every person, child or adult, wakes up with the option to be happy or sad. As Abraham Lincoln is credited with saying: *"You are as happy as you want to be."* This sounds like an overly simple "fortune cookie" philosophy, but it's actually brilliant.

We each have personal control whether we are happy or sad, despite what others may do or say to us. It's common for a child to think, "I'd be happy if only..." The "if only" might be having a certain friend, new cell phone, the most popular jeans or tennis shoes, a car, less acne, et cetera. But we can demonstrate how happiness has nothing to do with popularity, beauty, having lots of possessions, or all the things we think dictate our happiness.

For example, you only need to look in the news to see how some of the youngest and most beautiful celebrities, who have everything a person could hope for in life, are clearly sad by their self-destructive behavior (drugs, suicide, arrests). And to the contrary, there are people all over the world with barely enough to live on, and living a hard life, who start each day with a smile. Happiness and self-respect comes from inside ourselves and is a conscious decision.

Do we want to start our day with a smile or a frown? Do we want to be in control of our own emotional destiny, or let others control it for us? Helping your child embrace this philosophy, and see you living it as well, will go a long way toward them finding contentment not only as a child, but later as an adult as well.

Don't be afraid to refer to your stepchild as "my son" or my daughter."

If it feels right, say it. Maybe your stepchild is waiting for you to make the "first move" in eliminating the "step" from your vocabulary. Make it a casual reference, where they overhear you talking about them, maybe proudly talking about their positive actions or effort in something, instead of making a big production about it. "My son, Jimmy, learned to ride his bike this weekend!"

You will get cues from them if they like it or not, so go with the flow either way. If they indicate they don't like that, don't get offended, just ask how they'd like to be referred to. Maybe say, "I think of you as my son, so I call you that. But I won't if you don't like it." And don't give up. If it feels right for another try in a year or two, go for it.

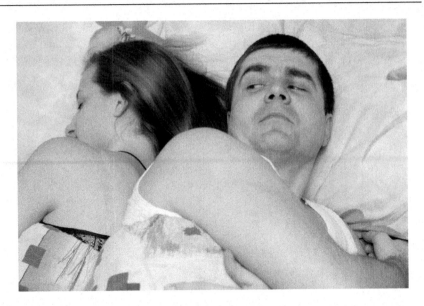

DO be prepared for the sex with your spouse to change.

On the one hand, most couples in second marriages usually find the sex more satisfying with their new spouse. This is because each person has had more life experience to select the right spouse this time around, and was able to choose a partner whose attitudes and lifestyle better match their own.

The flip side is that often most of the sexual intimacy with you as the stepparent was in the pre-marriage dating realm, where each adult could focus on each other. But when the marriage occurs, the realities of daily life come into play: jobs, meeting the needs of the kids, yard/house work, et cetera. Suddenly the sex diminishes and "family life" takes over. Jealousy by the stepparent over the existing parent spending so much time with the child is often not far behind.

It's understandable that usually a couple's sex life will not match the key and vigorous role it played in the very beginning of the relationship. But still, as a relationship matures and adjusts, a happy marriage usually requires a happy bedroom. Early communication with each other about feeling neglected in the bedroom is key, whether this feeling comes from the husband or the wife. And talking specifically over bedroom desires should not be taboo.

Don't brush aside your child's grief.

A child will grieve for the loss of a parent, whether because of death, abandonment, or even if that parent is living across town due to divorce (still lost to the child on a daily basis as a parent). This is also often true even if the absent parent was of terrible character and a poor parent. There is a sense of loss regardless.

Well-intentioned but misguided people gloss over the pain and try to help with comments like "She/he was never there for you anyway," "You are better off now that he/she is gone," or "Better to live in a happy home than one where parents were always arguing."

Those statements may be completely true, but truth does not take away grief or the sense of loss, particularly for a child. And even if one of the reasons for the split between parents was for the child's welfare, a child is generally not going to understand this.

The reality is your child can go through a grief cycle similar to what you likely first felt when you knew the relationship was ending. Even with the maturity of being an adult, you likely had a tough time with those emotions. So imagine dealing with those same emotions as a child.

There is often an initial stage of shock and denial, followed by anger (coupled with frustration as the child recognizes their lack of power to stop the ending of their family), then comes the grief.

Sometimes misguided guilt can contribute toward a child's grief. Make sure they know they had nothing to do with the breakup. Free them from any potential feelings of responsibility by making sure they know they did not cause the problem, nor could they solve it for you.

To help your child through grief and toward acceptance, don't let them put their lives "on hold." Instead, stick to normal routines and everyday life. This is very, very important. It's all too easy to let a child stay away from normal activities. More than anything, your compassion and patience is needed. If your child is letting you witness their grief and loss, the good news is they trust you enough to share it, and want your emotional support. Grieving together, rather than alone, can be easier.

DO be prepared for a child's rejection.

It's easy to think that a stepparent will be welcomed as the family hero, particularly if the out-of-house parent (usually the dad) abandoned the family and all his responsibilities, and you voluntarily step in to fill them. You may secretly feel you should get a pat on the back, but you likely will not get one, particularly from the child, at least not initially.

Children sometimes think that they themselves are responsible for the parent's out-of-house parent's absence: "Dad didn't have a job and babies are expensive, so he left," or "Mom didn't love me enough so she didn't want to see me anymore." A child may think things will change and the parent will return, but not if the child has given their love to a new parent taking their place. So their love for you is withheld to keep the door open for the absent parent to return. This involves time and patience on your part.

It is also possible that a child may have come to grips with a parent leaving, but doesn't feel safe in giving love, thinking that the last dad or mom left, so why risk loving you when you might do the same. Countless assurances may not convince them otherwise.

The old saying of "just showing up is half of parenting" is a true one. The longer you are there through good times and bad, and the more you are demonstrating day-by-day, moment-by-moment, that you will not be disappearing when things get tough, the sooner you will be allowed more fully into their hearts.

Do be prepared for your stepchild to badmouth you to the out-of-house parent.

It can be very hurtful for you to have found an enjoyable activity, let's say stepdad and son playing catch in the backyard. Then you hear from the out-of-house parent or another person that the child said he actually hates playing catch with you: "It's stupid" and you "throw like a girl."

What is usually happening is that the child feels loyalty for the out-of-house parent, and guilt over enjoying time with you. By badmouthing something he actually enjoys doing with you, in the child's mind he or she is just showing loyalty to the out-of-house parent. In a way, it is almost an admirable quality, that sense of loyalty. So your reaction is to do and say nothing. Just keep offering to play catch (or whatever the activity is), until the child actually says he doesn't want to. The reality is, he is likely enjoying himself.

Don't defend yourself against every negative comment about you from the out-of-house parent.

Sadly, some relationships that have ended never really end. This is because one or both parties continue to bear bad feelings and have an irresistible desire that everyone see the situation as they do. And sometimes stepparents in particular get even more venom from the out-of-house parent.

Kids are often put in the middle of this, hearing negative comments about a parent and/or stepparent from the out-of-house parent. While it is worth an attempt to privately and peacefully discuss the detriment to the child in this negativity with the out-of-house parent, some exes will continue down this destructive path.

As the stepparent, avoid the knee-jerk reaction to cut loose with a matching reply to the child: "He says *I've* got a lousy job? Well at least I *have* a job. He can't even afford his child support payments."

Even if what you say is 100% true, you will not impress your stepchild by criticizing the out-of-house parent (even if the child secretly agrees with you). What *will* impress your child is your maturity and emotional stability. Instead try, "Oh, I'm sorry he feels that way. I'll just keep doing the best I can." Then move on, "So... how was school today?"

As hard as it is to want to defend yourself, a child on his or her own will figure out when one parent is dishonest in what he or she tells the child. Kids are experts and spotting false comments and self-serving commentary.

DO help your child buy gifts for the out-of-house parent.

You are a stepmom and your stepchild's out-of-house mother has a birthday coming up. Show your support for their relationship, and your confidence in your own relationship with the child, and either remind the child about the upcoming birthday, or even better, go out and buy the gift together.

Hopefully the out-of-house parent is showing that same sensitivity to you. But if not, your child will eventually recognize the difference between your unselfish behavior, and the lack of it by the out-of-house parent. You are not showing this kindness to the out-of-house parent to win a

70

"kindness contest" and impress your child, but simply because this kind of behavior is good for your child and the extended family relationship.

Do understand the reason for a child's anger and rudeness.

Whether because the absent parent disappointed them with their failure to continue parenting, or simply because a child is slow to trust, often acting out is a child really asking "Does he or she love me enough to put up with me?"

You are undergoing such "trust" checks every day and you need to be up to the challenge. That doesn't mean you let rudeness go unchecked, or bad behavior go without consequences, but you do so calmly and fairly. You make it clear you are disappointed in their behavior, but you love them.

Don't "pass the buck" to the stepparent.

There is a natural inclination to want to avoid making tough decisions, or where you know your answer will make your child mad at you. For example, your daughter wants to go out on her first date and you think she's not ready, or you have conditions. Or your son wants to spend the night at a friend's home where you don't feel good about the parental supervision, or the character of the other kids in attendance.

Particularly when you want to say "no," don't answer your child's request with "Let me ask your stepmom/dad." This puts the burden on the stepparent, who is already most vulnerable to the child's criticism. And admit it, you are really stalling for time to deliver the "no," or you don't want to be the one to face your child's disappointment.

Instead simply say, "Let me think about it and we'll talk about it later today / tomorrow." In this way you as the existing parent are taking primary responsibility. This is not to say your child can't know you will later be discussing the issue with the stepparent, as that should be the case in all major parenting decisions, but you don't need to make the decision be seen as primarily that of the stepparent. And if the answer to your child's request is "no," it should most often be you who delivers it, not the stepparent.

Don't let your guilt over a failed marriage make you spoil your child.

You were married to a good person, but it just didn't work out. There can often be guilt associated with your decision which resulted in removing the child's father or mother from their daily lives. Perhaps you think "I took their father/mother away from them." Or even if you don't think so, your child might feel that way, and throw it in your face at every opportunity.

You can't let this change the way you need to parent, however. The result will only be a spoiled child, and you being seen as easily manipulated. It's one thing to understand and be sympathetic to the pain of a child regarding their absent parent, but that is not an excuse to let bad behavior occur without an appropriate discussion or consequence. Nor do you want to soften every sad moment with a gift.

Don't control your kids. Guide them.

Kids resent being told what to do, particularly when it feels to them it happens all day long; first at home, then at school, then later by a coach or after-school activities leader. And being told by a stepparent may feel especially unwelcome. Your goal as a parent is not simply to get your children to do what you want, rather to guide them to become self-motivated, high-functioning adults, respecting themselves and others, and eventually becoming a positive force in the world.

It is true that you may make your personal day easier by simply ordering your child to do certain tasks, at certain times, and in certain ways. ("You *will* do your homework the minute you get home from school and you will *not* get up from the dining room table until it's done. No friends, no

TV.") But issuing such orders does not empower your child in any way, or truly teach responsibility, just how to follow orders.

Instead try, "Your homework needs to be all done before 8:00 o'clock tonight, so make sure you leave enough time after you play with Joey after school." And rather than an order like "Bring a jacket. It will get cold later," try a question, "What is the weather going to be later? Do you think you need a jacket?"

And if they make the wrong decision, let them bear the consequences. (They declined a jacket, so they will have to deal with being cold all day. They forgot their lunch yet again, so they will be hungry during lunchtime at school). And you will be extra wise to not bring up the bad decision later with an "I told you so." Instead say nothing and let the natural consequence from their decision be their lesson. Hopefully they will be more likely to listen the next time you ask a question intended to make them think for themselves, such as "Do you think you need a jacket?" or "If you do that activity will you be able to finish your homework by 8:00 o'clock?"

DO recognize your stepchild may show love in different ways.

You may be sad your stepchild has not yet said "I love you." But everyone, and particularly children, shows their love and affection differently.

For example, you might be very verbal, and be used to a lot of giving and receiving of "I love you." But maybe your stepchild is not so verbally oriented. Perhaps he or she feels more comfortable sitting on your lap and snuggling while reading a book. Or maybe it's not even physical. Perhaps it's dedicating time and making craft projects for you, or asking to share time with you in activities like baking cookies.

Be grateful for any such signs of affection and don't demand that the child's method of showing affection matches yours.

Do use the fewest words possible.

As adults, we love to talk, and talk. And talk. So when we feel a child needs advice or information, we can't wait to share our wisdom. But kids, even older ones in their teens, need it short. Their interest tends to wane the more words are spoken. Worse of all, the intended message is diluted by all the excess words.

A good plan is to strive for a short answer, as in under one minute. And if they have questions about it, they'll ask, and you start the one-minute clock again. If they don't ask questions, you likely gave them what they needed to know.

Don't criticize a child for bad behavior, criticize the behavior itself.

When we criticize someone, especially kids, our message is often unfortunately interpreted as "You are bad," "You are a failure," or "You are a disappointment." So rather than words that say, "*You* were bad," try words that instead say, "Your *behavior* was bad."

Perhaps a disappointing report card is being discussed. So instead of "You were a terrible student to get three Ds on your report card," consider, "I don't think your effort and study habits were very good to get these grades. Let's discuss how we can change that." The first statement is saying "you are a bad student," but the second is saying "your study habits are bad." One is commenting on the person and one is addressing the behavior.

Do respect a stepchild's need for privacy and decorum.

You are a stepdad and your stepdaughter is a rapidly developing teenager. When she was four she'd run naked in the backyard through the sprinklers. Now she's conscious of her body and wants privacy. Whether you are the existing parent or the stepparent, you need to understand and respect these desires for private bathroom time, and knocking and waiting for a "come in" before entering the child's bedroom.

And this also applies to the parent and stepparent's body and manner of dress. Stepdad likes to wake up Saturday morning and make breakfast for the family in his boxers. Or maybe stepmom likes to wear a little nightie around the house at night. Maybe that was fine when the kids were little, but as children get more attuned to sexuality, they may become uncomfortable with the stepparent or existing parent being too casual with their dress. Respect the kids' feelings, even if you feel they are overly sensitive in their feelings.

Don't feel every holiday must be spent together.

Almost every family has had battles over where to spend holidays. Different sets of relatives live far apart, and maybe that means having to choose only one to visit, or you visit both, but it requires a long day in the car.

This dynamic is only more complicated with a stepfamily, as there are now double the relatives, and conflicting existing traditions on how to spend holidays. Maybe your wife and her child have visited grandma and grandpa for Thanksgiving at their farm 100 miles away from home every year since the child was born. And you and your child have a tradition to go skiing for a four-day weekend over Thanksgiving at a resort to gather with your parents and siblings.

It's perfectly fine to sometimes go your separate ways for holidays. With families often extended over great distances, it's just a reality. So rather than make one side of the family miss their trip to grandma and grandpa's for Thanksgiving, or the family ski trip, or make everyone miserable stuck in a car all day to cover too much territory, wish each other well and enjoy your time each doing exactly what you want. Plus, dragging along unwilling participants means not only will they not have fun, but they will likely take away everyone else's enjoyment as well.

From the Author

Thanks so much for reading *STEPPARENTING: 50 One-Minute DOs & DON'Ts for Stepdads & Stepmoms*. Taking the time to learn more about effective stepparenting (and parenting in general) shows how much you care about being the best possible parent. As the saying goes, "It takes a village to raise a child," but as parents we are the chiefs of that village.

Personally, I hate instructional or motivational books that are hundreds of pages in length, and by the time I finish, I realize they could have summarized the important parts into just a few pages. I don't know if books are like that because people wrongly think "weight equals wisdom," or so publishers can charge more for books. And even worse than that is the result of overly long books. I don't know about you, but many times I start a book, but it is so long and cumbersome that I give up before I ever finish, so my time was wasted.

So I tried to make this book short, insightful and helpful for real day-to-day life. I imagine when you read these fifty DOs and DON'Ts, that with some you said, "That's great advice, but I already knew that." And also likely sometimes, "I did know that, but I realize I'm not doing it." (If so, I'm proud to be your reminder.)

But hopefully there were several DOs and DON'Ts that you had not thought about, or which gave you some new insight. Even one helpful tip – or to look at in the reverse, one continued mistake in parenting that is not corrected - can make a huge difference in your relationship with your stepchild.

If you have a comment or question, I'd enjoy hearing from you at Randy@RandallHicks.com. I respond to all emails. Perhaps you will even have a suggestion to improve a future edition of this book.

Again, thanks for reading. I sincerely hope you will take a moment to review this book online on Amazon or other online retailer so others looking for help in stepparenting can hear from real parents and stepparents in finding helpful resources. So many books on the subject read like a college textbook or a social worker manual. I hope I've made this book fun, easily readable, with tips ready to instantly put into action.

Best wishes,

About the Author

Randall Hicks is an attorney and author. He has written informational books regarding both adoption and parenting, as well as several novels and one children's book.

His books have been featured on many national TV shows (*The Today Show, CBS This Morning, The Home Show, Sally Jesse Raphael, Mike & Maty, John and Leeza from Hollywood*, on the PBS network, and more) as well as in the print media (*The New York Times, Chicago Sun Times, Los Angeles Times* and more).

Randy limits his practice to adoption, specifically stepparent adoption, and is the founder of The Stepparent Adoption Center (StepparentAdoptionCenter.com). He lives in California and has offices in Riverside, Orange and San Diego Counties. He is the proud father of his children, Ryan and Hailey, now young adults.

CPSIA information can be obtained
at www.ICGtesting.com
Printed in the USA
LVOW01s1800010317
525811LV00011B/1114/P

9 780979 443039